SURVIVAL IN THE RAINFOREST

John and Sue Erbacher

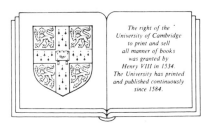

The right of the
University of Cambridge
to print and sell
all manner of books
was granted by
Henry VIII in 1534.
The University has printed
and published continuously
since 1584.

CAMBRIDGE UNIVERSITY PRESS
CAMBRIDGE
NEW YORK   PORT CHESTER   MELBOURNE   SYDNEY

Published by the Press Syndicate of the University of Cambridge
The Pitt Building, Trumpington Street, Cambridge CB2 1RP, UK
40 West 20th Street, New York, NY 10011, USA
10 Stamford Road, Oakleigh, Melbourne 3166, Australia

© Cambridge University Press 1991
First published 1991

Printed in Hong Kong by Colorcraft Ltd

National Library of Australia cataloguing in publication data

Erbacher, John, 1951– .
    Survival in the rainforest.
    ISBN 0 521 40290 5

[1]. Aborigines, Australian — Hunting. [2]. Aborigines,
Australian — Food. [3]. Aborigines, Australian —
Implements. [4]. Aborigines, Australian — Fishing. 5.
Rain forests — Australia. I. Erbacher, Sue,
1949– .

994.0049915

British Library cataloguing in publication data

Erbacher, John 1951– .
    Survival in the rainforest.
    1. Australian aborigines
    I. Title
    994.0049915
    ISBN 0-521-40290-5

Library of Congress cataloguing in publication data

Erbacher, John, 1951– .
    Survival in the rainforest/John and Sue Erbacher.
        p.   cm.
    Summary: Describes how the Kuku-Yalanji Aborigines hunt, fish,
and gather and prepare food in the Australian rainforest.
    ISBN 0-521-40290-5
    1. Kuku-Yalanji (Australian people) — Juvenile literature. 2. Rain
forest ecology — Australia — Queensland — Juvenile literature.
[1. Kuku-Yalanji (Australian people) 2. Australian aborigines.
3. Rain forests — Australia.] I. Erbacher, Sue, 1949– .
II. Title.
DU125.K75E74   1991
994.3'6 — dc20   90-49276

Kuku-Yalanji People
The Gorge
North Queensland

15 April 1990

John and Sue have been our friends for a long time now. They have been spending their holidays with us for about seventeen years and we always look forward to them.

They always take pictures and films of people here at the Gorge and we think they are very good pictures which show our way of living and we are very proud of this. We shared planning and discussion about the pictures with John and Sue and the things we helped them put on films.

We've seen the films lots of times and they give a true story of ourselves in our own country. It is good these stories and pictures in the books *Aborigines of the rainforest* and *Survival in the rainforest* give people opportunities to see what we are doing and we like to say also that we are only too pleased to have John and Sue take our pictures and tell our stories and we hope to have them take some more of us.

These pictures and stories: we are pleased for them to be shown to other people.

Yours sincerely

David Buchanan
Beverly Buchanan
Harry McNamara
Eileen McNamara
Norman C. Walker
Wilma Walker

PREFACE

Since 1973 we have been filming the Kuku-Yalanji Aborigines of northern Queensland. We have made seventeen 16mm films on Aboriginal tribal life which provide a valuable record of Kuku-Yalanji traditions and customs. The filming was done over a long period of time which meant that we gained the confidence of the Aborigines and the opportunity to be shown seasonal activities and events which are not normally accessible to other people. You must have a long-established friendship with the Aborigines before they feel comfortable about sharing certain experiences and information with you.

During the last eleven years, in addition to making films, we have travelled throughout Victoria showing these films and lecturing in schools and other institutions.

John and Sue Erbacher
Hervey Bay, Queensland

ACKNOWLEDGEMENT

The authors wish to thank the Kuku-Yalanji people for their valuable assistance. Without their help this book would not have been possible.

CONTENTS

THE KUKU–YALANJI TRIBE

The Kuku-Yalanji is a tribe of over five hundred Aborigines who live in the tropical rainforests of northern Queensland, Australia. Their tribal area extends along the coast from Mossman to Cooktown, and inland to the Palmer River and Mount Carbine. The Kuku-Yalanji are the only remaining tribal rainforest people in Australia who still retain their own language and culture.

The people have an extraordinary knowledge of the skills needed to live off the land and are expert in hunting, food gathering, medicine, and in the making of weapons and implements. This knowledge and experience, gained over hundreds of years, has equipped the tribe in the art of survival, bringing it through times of prosperity and hardship.

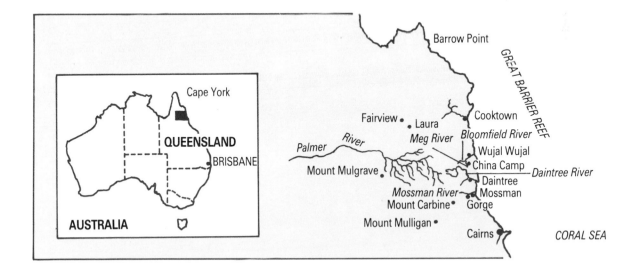

BUSH FOOD — PLANTS

The rainforest provides a large variety of food for the Kuku-Yalanji people throughout the year. Trees, vines, and other plants provide fruit, nuts, berries, stems, roots and bulbs. Some of these include wild raspberries, wild ginger, white apples, cassowary plums, forest pandanus, wait-a-while berries, walking-stick palm fruit, daintree nuts, bush bananas, quandongs, zamia nuts and different types of yams. Some food is poisonous and must be treated before it can be eaten.

The centre of the top section of the trunk of some palm trees can be eaten. It is called the cabbage and is considered a delicacy. When the forest pandanus ripens it can be broken open by hand and eaten. The flesh tastes like a mixture of jelly and icecream.

Cauliflory, found only in tropical rainforests, occurs when the flowers and fruit develop on the trunk of the tree. One species is called white apples by the Aborigines.

There are two types of wild ginger, 'jidu' and 'junjun'. The fruits of both types grow at the base of the plant. Junjun resembles a clump of small, green, spiky balls and jidu, a group of red and white flower buds. The leaves of jidu are used for wrapping up meat before it is cooked in hot coals. The people believe that if wild ginger is picked before it is ripe, storms will result. Young children are sometimes blamed for causing unseasonal rain.

A white edible clay called 'kambar' is also eaten. Kambar is highly addictive in the same way coffee is and is not eaten regularly. It is prepared by hanging it in a dillybag over the fire so that it absorbs flavours from the food being cooked.

BUSH FOOD — ANIMALS

A wide variety of animals, reptiles, birds, insects, and grubs is eaten. These include kangaroos, wallabies, possums, echidnas, wild pigs, goannas, pythons, cassowaries, scrub hens, scrub turkeys and green ants. One favourite is the witchetty grub which is very scarce and hard to find. It is so tasty it is rarely shared. Eggs and wild honey are also much sought after.

'Kumbi', the flying fox, is occasionally speared and eaten. It has cape-like wings, and its name, kumbi, is also used to describe European clothing, especially shirts and dresses. Snakes are still eaten but they are not as popular as they were in the past.

The Aborigines like to collect and eat the eggs of the scrub hen. The scrub hen's nest consists of a mound of leaves and sticks measuring up to three metres high and seven metres across. The eggs must be located and dug out. They are then baked in the coals of a fire or boiled in a bark container filled with water. The eggs are eaten at all stages of incubation.

Echidna is regarded as a delicacy. The flesh of the echidna resembles pork in texture and taste. It is generally reserved for the older people because of its quality and tenderness, although some of them are barred by tribal lore from eating it.

Pregnant women are not allowed to eat certain foods, such as cassowary meat, because of the effect it is believed to have on the unborn child. The Aborigines believe that if a pregnant woman eats cassowary meat, her child is likely to be born with a humped back.

Food from the sea and rivers includes fish, turtles, crabs, prawns, shellfish, tortoises and shrimps.

YAMS

A plentiful supply of various kinds of yam is found in the tropical rainforest. The yam plant is a vine and climbs vigorously up trees although the fruit grows underground.

The Aborigines find the vine with its distinctive heart-shaped leaves, then follow its growth to where it goes into the ground. A digging stick or the sharp end of a woomera is used to dig the yam out. Aborigines always replant the growing end of the vine to make sure there will be yams again the following year.

Yams vary in size and, if left to mature, can grow to almost the size of a person. Some varieties of yam commonly used include the white yam, the purple yam and 'wukay', the hairy yellow yam.

The white yam is easily identified by its big green leaves. It grows very big and when cooked it resembles mashed potato.

The purple yam is identified by its purple vine and purple veins in its leaves. This is a smaller variety of yam which, when broken or peeled, has a beautiful purple-coloured flesh. The yam retains its colour after it is cooked and tastes delicious.

HAIRY YAMS — 'WUKAY'

Yams must be identified correctly, as not all are safe to eat. 'Wukay', the hairy yam, is a poisonous variety which must be carefully treated before it can be eaten. Aborigines are very skilled in the art of making poisonous food safe to eat, and the process of making the poisonous yam edible is a lengthy one, taking more than a day.

The yam is cut into pieces and boiled in a billycan of water. A stick poked into the yam indicates whether it is properly cooked. Once cooked the skin can be peeled off easily with minimum wastage. The cooked pieces of yam are placed in a dillybag which is used as a strainer. With a billycan of water placed directly under the dillybag, the yam is squashed to a pulp and forced through the dillybag to settle in the billycan of water below. Any pieces of yam remaining in the dillybag cannot be processed and must be discarded. Once the mixture in the billycan is left to settle, poison begins to seep out of the yam into the water. The water is then poured off and some of the poison removed with it. This must be done gently so that the yam pulp, now settled at the bottom, is not disturbed. This washing process is repeated many times until all the poison is removed. The mixture, which now contains little water, is left to settle for a few hours before it is poured into the dillybag and hung in a tree where it sets like a jelly overnight. Next morning the yam is ready to eat. Processed yam tastes similar to potato and is considered very good food by the Aborigines.

ZAMIA NUTS — 'MARRA'

Experience has taught the Kuku-Yalanji people how to survive in their land. They have learned which foods are safe to eat and which ones are poisonous. This bush knowledge is the people's cultural equivalent of European technology. The fruit of the zamia palm, called 'marra' by the people, is a poisonous nut. The early settlers called it 'rickety palm' after it poisoned the cattle, paralysing their hindquarters and causing them to stagger and reel and sometimes die.

The nuts are roasted in a fire before being cracked and shelled. The kernels are crushed between two stones and then put into a dillybag which is placed in a running stream and left overnight. The water washes the poison out of the nuts and by next morning they are safe to eat.

In the past this knowledge made the difference between members of the tribe going hungry and having something to eat in lean times.

COCONUTS — 'JIRIMANDI'

Coconut palms grow in abundance in northern Queensland. Attaining a height of thirty metres, these palms bear fruit of different sizes and colours, including green, yellow, and orange. When fully ripe the coconut turns brown.

The people eat the coconut at various stages of its growth. Ripe coconuts fall off the trees and need only to be collected. More mature coconuts will have shoots growing out of their husks. These contain an inner kernel called the apple. The apple is soft and considered an even greater delicacy than the white meat. Green or immature coconuts are harder to obtain, since the trees have to be climbed and the nuts twisted on their stems to break them off.

Coconuts are husked using a spike as a lever. The coconut is pushed on to the spike and twisted sideways to tear off the thick fibrous husk. Removal of the husk reveals three eyes on the coconut's hard inner shell. These eyes can easily be pierced with a sharp object in order to drain the milk from the nut. The hard shell is then broken revealing the delicious white meat inside. The meat of a mature coconut is chewy and the milk is rich and tasty. When the nut is not fully ripe the milk is at its best. It has a slight fizz similar to lemonade.

BARK SHELTER — 'WURUN'

The Kuku-Yalanji make shelters, or 'wuruns', from bark cut from the turpentine and stringybark trees. The messmate tree is a source of bark also, but it is not as good since its bark cracks after being exposed to the weather.

Traditionally the bark is cut after the first big storms in October. The people believe that thunder and lightning cause the bark to loosen on the trees. The cutting begins in November and continues for as long as the bark is needed, or until winter, when the bark becomes tight on the trees again.

Bark is taken from a living tree in large pieces up to six metres in length. It is then heated over a fire and bent over the framework of the shelter. The frame for the shelter is made from thin flexible saplings which are bent into a semi-circular shape. Straight saplings are tied horizontally across the framework using strips of lawyer cane. The pieces of bark are secured at the top by a sapling strapped horizontally along the ridge to hold them down. To secure the remainder of the bark, small holes are punched through it so that the bark can be tied to the framework with lawyer-cane binding.

Smoke from the fire helps to cure the bark and timber, which means the shelter lasts a long time. The framework eventually rots away and is replaced, but the original bark is kept.

Bark shelters were built as permanent dwellings. In different seasons the people travelled, but they often returned to these permanent shelters.

Because of its coolness the fan-palm shelter is used mainly as a summer home. It is quick to build but lasts only one season.

These shelters can be made in different shapes, with either a rectangular or circular floor. The main section of the frame is made from saplings pushed into the ground and bent over in a semi-circular shape. Beginning at the top, and working towards the bottom of the frame, lawyer-cane bands are laid horizontally around the framework and tied to the saplings to hold them in place. These lawyer-cane bands are positioned at regular intervals down the sides.

Fan-palm leaves are used as thatching. The natural shape of the leaf resembles the open position of a fan. The leaves are closed up by hand, arranged as thatching, and tied to the frame using strips of lawyer cane.

Bark is pulled off the paperbark tree, and this is laid on the floor to make a soft mattress.

In the open forest, where lawyer cane does not grow, the people use thin saplings to tie the framework together and to hold the thatching down. In areas where there are no fan palms, blady grass is used as thatching. In the past, when the Aborigines practised regular burning of the country, blady grass was more plentiful than fan-palm leaves.

A fire is built at the entrance of the shelter and this is used for warmth, cooking, and as a deterrent to mosquitoes.

IRONWOOD GLUE

The ironwood tree — 'jujubala' — has always been of great value to the Aborigines in northern Queensland as it is the source of a valuable glue.

The roots must be cut from living trees so only one root is taken from a single tree. If a large quantity of glue is required additional roots are taken from other trees. It is very important to the Aborigines that the trees survive.

The glue-making process must be completed when the root is freshly cut. The root is heated over a fire, causing the sap in the bark to bubble into a black, resinous substance. The resin is scraped off the root and placed on the end of a stick and then reheated over the fire. Using the back of an axe, the resin is then pounded against a log to form a better consistency. The result is a strong, black-coloured glue which is soft and workable when hot, but which sets hard upon cooling. The glue is formed into a lump and this is reheated when it is needed.

Ironwood glue is used as an all-purpose glue, and is particularly useful when making woomeras and fish spears. For centuries this substance has provided the Aborigines with a form of hard-setting, resinous glue which has a durability and smoothness similar to modern glues. It can also be used as an additive and mixed with other glues of lesser quality to improve their strength.

BLACK PALM — 'DUWAR'

The black palm is of great value to the Kuku-Yalanji people. This rare species of palm, found only in tropical rainforests, grows to a height of thirty metres with a trunk diameter of just twenty centimetres. The wood is so hard that it can bend the edge of an axe blade so a lot of time and energy must be expended before the tree can be cut through. The bottom section of the black palm splits lengthwise quite easily, and this hard, straight-grained wood is used for making spears. To increase its hardness even further, the point of the spear is heated over a fire. Because of its strength, black palm also makes a good peg for the end of the woomera.

The black palm is used in a particular way by the women of the tribe. The top section of the trunk is made up of many sheaths, and these provide the women with a strong, durable fibre for dillybags.

Black-palm music sticks are sometimes used in corroborees. When tapped together the sticks produce a distinct metallic sound.

The nulla nulla is another product of the black palm. This is essentially a hunting weapon, often used in the dense parts of the forest where other weapons would be a hindrance. The nulla nulla is thrown underarm across the top of the ground, often at small animals. It hits the animal in the legs, throwing it off balance. This allows the hunter to run and catch it by hand.

The black palm is also used to make digging sticks. Digging sticks resemble double-pointed spears and are used for digging yams and other underground food. The use of hard black palm means that the digging stick remains sharp throughout prolonged use under all conditions.

PIG HUNTING

The pig is an introduced species to the rainforest. There is no Kuku-Yalanji name for it so the Aborigines refer to it as 'piggy'.

Pig hunting is a way of life with the Kuku-Yalanji people. The hunt usually takes place within the rainforest, where a group of hunters, with their dogs, search for the fresh trail of a pig. These days the dogs scent out the pig and then grab it by the snout or ears and pull it down. The hunter then comes up and kills it with a knife or rifle.

Wild boars are dangerous. If cornered, a wild pig will often charge at the hunter or his dog, causing severe injury with its sharp tusks. Hunting dogs frequently bear scars due to encounters with wild pigs. Sometimes they are even killed in the fight.

After the pig is captured it is cut up. The head and insides are discarded and the carcass cut into equal portions so that each hunter carries the same weight. Sometimes the hunters have to walk across kilometres of rough country to bring the pig back to camp. The hunters refuse to bring back a pig which is thin or sickly. They attribute such conditions to evil spirits, and therefore automatically protect themselves against parasites and diseases.

Back at camp the hunter may not do as he chooses with his catch. Close relatives are receivers of certain sections of wild game caught by the hunter, and various portions are reserved for them as their right due to their relationship to the hunter.

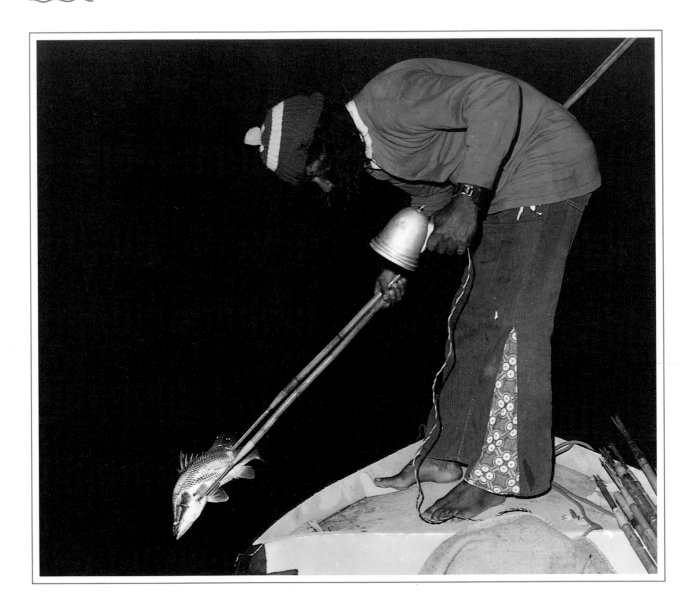

FISHING

The warm tropical waters of the Great Barrier Reef abound with fish. In the darkness of the night many deep-water fish swim to the shallows to feed. The coastal Aborigines have been aware of these feeding habits for many years and they use this knowledge to advantage.

Using a boat, a spotlight and spears, Aborigines row quietly over the reef at low tide in search of fish. The fisherman at the bow uses a spotlight to locate the fish, while the oarsman manoeuvres the boat so it is close enough for the fish to be speared. Frequently a strong, fighting fish will swim off with a spear in its back which means a second or even a third spear must be thrown.

Sometimes red reflector tape is used on the ends of the spears. This glows in the beam of the spotlight which helps to locate the spear again in the dark. Fish are detected sometimes by a ripple on the surface of the water, but often the fish's eyes give it away. In the beam from the spotlight the eyes, in a certain position, glow red or silver. While some fish are frightened off by the hunter's advance, others are attracted to the light and can swim right up to the side of the boat. If this happens escape is unlikely; the fish spear is known to be a deadly weapon in the hands of a Kuku-Yalanji tribesman.

STINGRAY — 'YAWU'

A shallow-water delicacy is 'yawu', the stingray. Stingrays are speared using a fish spear and woomera. This fish has a poisonous barb half-way along its tail but the Aborigines know how to remove it safely. With the spear in its body, and the end of its tail gripped firmly between the hunter's teeth, the tail is stretched tightly so that the stingray cannot lash about. This leaves the hunter's right hand free to break off the barb. The stingray is then killed by being hit several times over the head with the woomera.

Back at camp a special process is used to remove the strong taste from the stingray's flesh. The liver is taken out and kept until later. The liver indicates the health of the fish, and some fish are discarded untouched. The flaps and body are then cut up and boiled. When cooled, the skin and bones are removed from the flesh. The shredded flesh is then put into a calico bag, and water is poured through it to remove the strong taste. Finally the stingray flesh is fried with its own liver, a process to which its superior flavour is attributed.

Stingray is much sought after by the people, although those who live in the Bloomfield River area are barred by tribal lore from eating it.

TURTLES — 'NGAWIYA'

Turtles are taken at sea with harpoons. They are hunted in the shallow waters along the coast and around the islands. In Queensland waters turtles are protected, and only Aborigines with special permits are allowed to hunt them. Hunting methods have changed over the years. Instead of using dugout canoes and paddles, these days Aborigines usually use boats with outboard motors.

Method of capture is simple. When the turtle is sighted it is chased by the hunters in their motor-powered boat. The hunter with the harpoon stands at the bow and points the way for the boat operator. Shallow water is essential as the turtle must be kept in sight. When the boat comes within range, the harpoon is thrown at the turtle and, if a hit is made, the harpoon's detachable head, with the rope attached, penetrates the hard shell while the heavy four-metre shaft floats off. The turtle is then hauled to the boat using the rope.

Another method used is to chase the turtle and force it to keep swimming, allowing it no time for life-giving breaths of air. When the turtle slows down to a more leisurely pace, the hunter at the bow of the boat dives over to grab the exhausted turtle by its shell.

There are three species of turtles found in Queensland waters, but the green turtle is the one most sought after for food. It is often prepared and cooked in the same way it was centuries ago, simmered in its shell in the coals of an open fire.

GREEN ANTS — 'YANGKA'

Green ants live in colonies and build nests of leaves stuck together with a white substance obtained from their larvae. Nests are found on bushes near the ground but can also be seen in trees up to twenty metres from the ground. If a nest is bumped thousands of green ants pour out, furiously attacking, biting, and stinging whatever may have disturbed their home. Fortunately their stinger cannot penetrate skin easily, although, if they do reach tender spots with their powerful nippers, break the skin and drop a spot of acid there, it is a very painful experience indeed.

Green ants, however, do have their uses. When a person has a cold the green ants are collected, squashed into a pulp and mixed with water. The mixture is either rubbed on the chest or drunk as a medicine.

The Kuku-Yalanji also eat the green ants. They provide a tasty snack for both children and hunters. In December the green ants' nests contain extra large larvae called 'kurrmaja' which later grow into drones. The nests are broken open and these larvae are eaten as well as the green ants. This is considered very good food. The larvae make excellent bait for fishing. When the fish are not biting, the people eat the bait instead.

STINGING TREE — 'MILI'

The deadly stinging tree provides its own cure if someone is stung by it. If brushed against, poisonous hairs on the leaves penetrate the skin of the victim. Death can result from extensive stinging, and severe pain from minor contact. Irritation can continue for weeks or months.

A cure is made by squashing the tree's berries and smearing the juice over the affected area. Once it becomes sticky it is scraped off with the blade of a knife. This removes most of the hairs and eases the pain.

RINGWORM CURE

The leaves of the six o'clock bush provide a cure for ringworm. The plant takes its name from the fact that, when darkness falls at six o'clock in the evening, the leaves fold in upon themselves and remain completely closed all night. This is the time the leaves must be picked. A leaf from the sandpaper fig is first rubbed over the area affected with ringworm to break up the surface of the skin, then the leaves of the six o'clock bush are squashed with a small amount of water and applied to the ringworm. A few days must elapse before the cure is complete, and during that time the patient must not wash the affected area. Sometimes this treatment needs to be repeated.

MAN SPEAR OR HUNTING SPEAR — 'DUWAR'

The man spear or hunting spear is a single-pointed weapon used for fighting and hunting wild animals, large birds, and snakes.

The spear is made from two pieces of wood. A heavy piece at the front of the spear and a light piece of wood at the back provide balance. This means that even if the spear is thrown crookedly it will straighten itself as it flies through the air.

Sometimes spears are fitted with barbs. These are usually made from stingray spikes or animal shinbones. Once the spear is made goanna fat or turtle oil is rubbed into the wood to preserve it.

In the past, using the man spear was the honourable way of settling disputes and fights. It rarely happened that more than one person was injured or killed in a fight. Usually, as soon as a person was wounded enough to drop to the ground, the debt was considered paid and the fight was finished.

Around the settlements and missions the carrying of these spears was banned. In time most of the people moved closer to the settlements and the hunting spear was, to a large extent, replaced by the rifle.

Peacemaker — Walmbaji

SPEAR FIGHTER — 'MALADIKARRA'

When an offence has been committed by a member of the tribe, the tribal elders determine the severity of the crime and then decide on a punishment. This could involve the offender having a certain number of spears thrown at him. He must then try to dodge and ward off the spears with his fighting woomera. If the person is not good at dodging spears, and if the type of offence allows it, he can call in a maladikarra, an expert spear fighter, to stand in for him. The maladikarra will do this for a close relative, or for payment. The maladikarra is skillful and unlikely to be injured. However, sometimes a penalty will consist of being speared in the leg or thigh, and the offender cannot escape this. In these situations a maladikarra cannot be used.

PEACEMAKER — 'WALMBAJI'

As the name suggests, the peacemaker is there to restore peace when fighting breaks out within the tribe. The peacemaker stands between the opposing parties and will stop the fight. If a man has lost a fight and is going to kill himself because of his loss of face, the peacemaker will intervene. If someone threatens to kill another person the peacemaker will step in and restrain them. No one loses face, as they have been prevented from carrying out the killing. The peacemaker is much respected and when he enters into a conflict nobody dares cause him injury or disobey him.

FISH SPEAR — 'KALKA'

The most important Aboriginal weapon is the fish spear. It is still extensively used and, because of this, the art of making this weapon has survived. The difference between the fish spear and the man spear is that the man spear has one point and the fish spear has a number of spikes.

Before white people came to the area, spear shafts were made from native bamboo or the spear stick tree called 'durral'. These spears were bigger and heavier than today's spears and were fitted with between four and six spikes made from hard wood, usually ironwood or black palm. The thirty-five centimetre long spikes had no barbs and were bound around the outside of the shaft. At the end of the spear the distance across the cluster of spikes was twenty-five centimetres.

Today the fish spear is made from lighter bamboo which grows in thickets along the river banks. The spear has three or more sharpened spikes made from welding rods or fencing wire, often with barbs. The spikes are fitted and glued into the shaft using a natural sap glue, then they are secured further by winding lawyer cane or some other binding around the outside of the shaft. Because the fish spear is such an effective weapon for catching fish, it will never become outdated. Children learn the skill of fish spearing at an early age and soon master it.

WOOMERA — 'MILBAYARR'

The woomera or spear thrower is used to throw spears.

A flat piece of wood about the length of a person's arm is used to make the woomera. A handle is shaped at one end, and at the other a peg is fitted neatly into a slot, where it is glued and bound with lawyer cane. The peg must be the strongest part of the woomera because it takes the full thrust of the spear. Therefore it is made with the toughest material available, usually black palm or ironwood. The end of the handle is often shaped like a round-ended spade and may be used as a digging tool.

The woomera extends the Aborigine's arm, giving extra leverage. This added power enables the Aborigine to throw the spear much further than he could without the woomera. The spear is usually thrown with relatively light force, but with a sharp flick of the wrist at the end of the throw. This increases the power and doubles the range of the spear. The woomera is not necessarily used to throw the spear a long distance, but rather to save the hunter's strength, or to throw the spear a short distance with plenty of hitting power. When fishing at close range the woomera is used only for spearing large fish. It is not used for small fish, because the force of the spear would immediately break the fish into pieces.

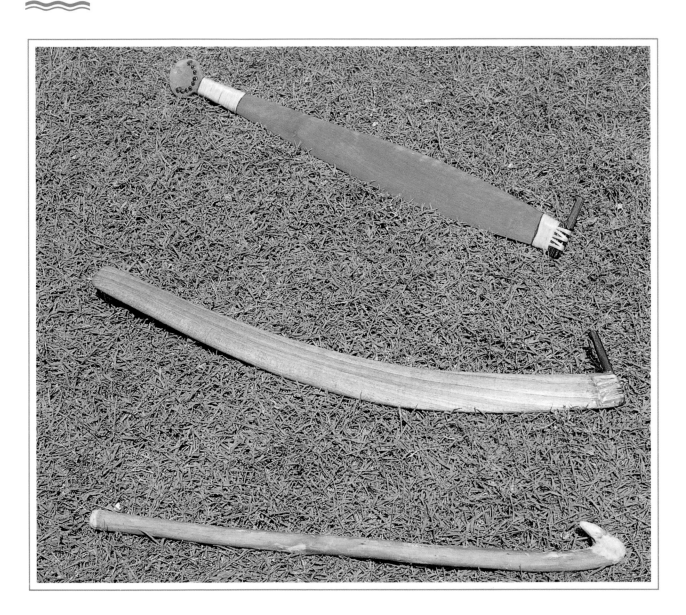

TYPES OF WOOMERAS

There are three types of woomeras used by the Kuku-Yalanji tribe. The fighting and hunting woomera, 'milbayarr', is a broad, straight woomera made from the spurwood tree. Spurwood is hard to cut, but easy to work into the required shape. The fighting woomera is decorated with bailer shell or gidgi seeds and its broad surface is useful for warding off spears during a fight. The hunting woomera is a less decorated, smaller version of the fighting woomera.

The fishing woomera, 'balur', is narrow and curved in shape and made from crow's foot wood. Its curved shape makes it more efficient when used in restricted areas, such as mangrove swamps.

The emergency woomera, 'bujilnga', can be made quickly from a branch of any type of tree. It is a good type of woomera for novices to use when learning the art of spear throwing.

When not in use the woomera was always placed in a certain position. Leaning against a tree or other object in a near vertical position, with the peg at the top, the woomera was always ready for use. In the event of a surprise attack the woomera could be picked up with one hand, the spear with the other and both could be put together and the spear launched in one fluid action. If a person was caught putting a woomera down in the wrong position the old people of the tribe would be angry at the offender.

BOOMERANG — 'WANGAL'

The boomerang has always been associated with the Australian Aborigines. Different types of boomerangs are used for different purposes, but perhaps the best known of these is the returning boomerang. This boomerang has the ability to come back to the thrower after having completed its flight of one or more circles. It is held in one hand with the blade pointing away from the thrower, and thrown with a spinning action into the wind. The blades are slightly twisted in opposite directions resembling the pitch of an aeroplane propeller. When the boomerang is thrown the spinning action pulls it through the air. The returning boomerang is a toy and not used in hunting.

In hunting, the killer boomerang is used. This non-returning boomerang is usually larger and not as curved as the returning boomerang. When thrown, the killer boomerang will not always kill the prey, but will often break the leg of an animal or the wing of a bird so that the hunter can catch it by hand.

Hook boomerangs are used as fighting sticks for hitting and throwing at people.

For best results boomerangs are carved from tree buttresses or bent tree roots. By using a bent tree root, strength is added to the boomerang since the wood grain follows the curve from one end to the other. An axe is often used to rough out the boomerang, then a piece of sharp, broken glass is used as a scraper in the final smoothing process.

DIDGERIDOO — 'YIKI YIKI'

The musical instrument, the didgeridoo, is a hollow pipe which, when blown into, produces various droning sounds. It is made from a narrow tree trunk. While the tree is still living, ants and termites eat out the centre, then build their nests in the hollow. At a later date the trunk is cut down and a sharp stick rammed down the middle to remove the nests. The trunk is then painted with ochre and ready to use.

The didgeridoo is played by placing the mouth against one end, and vibrating air between closed lips into the didgeridoo. This produces the distinctive droning sound. The differently pitched notes are made by altering the shape of the lips while blowing. To play the didgeridoo continuously the player must be able to breathe in through his nose and blow out through his mouth at the same time. This is not easily done although it looks simple, and it is difficult to find a skilled didgeridoo player.

FIRE STICKS — 'JIMAL'

The art of rubbing two sticks together to make fire is a skill which has always fascinated people. Although the Aborigines normally use matches to start fires, the art of making fires with fire sticks has not been lost.

Not just any type of wood can be used for fire sticks. The people obtain their fire sticks from a special tree which they call 'durral', the fire-stick tree.

One stick is placed horizontally on the ground, then a shallow hollow is cut in it. Into the side of this hollow is cut a notch which will act as a drain. The second stick is slightly green, and one end is shaped into a rounded point. This stick is held vertically with the rounded end placed in the hollow of the horizontal stick. Then it is twisted between the hands so that it rotates both clockwise and anti-clockwise with a drill-like motion. The vertical stick is twisted very fast and a heavy downward pressure is exerted at the same time. This action produces friction and heat. White smoke appears and soon black ash runs out of the drain on to a cushion of very fine grass which has been placed at the side. The ash is called tinder, which will glow red when it becomes hot. By surrounding the ash with more fine grass and then fanning it in the breeze, the grass soon bursts into flames. For an experienced Aborigine this process takes about half a minute.

DILLYBAGS — 'BALJI'

The dillybag resembles a shopping basket, and is used mainly for processing poisonous food. It is also used as a container for collecting nuts, berries, shellfish, and other small items of food. Large-size dillybags have been used for carrying babies.

Dillybags are made each year by the women at the beginning of the wet season in readiness for the ripening of 'wukay', the hairy yam. Wukay is a poisonous variety of yam which must be treated before it can be eaten. The dillybag is used as a strainer during this process. Other poisonous foods are also treated using a dillybag.

The fibre used for making dillybags comes from the top section of the black palm. This part of the tree is made up of many sheaths which can be peeled off like the layers of an onion. Each sheath consists of many strong fibres surrounded by a soft pithy substance. The women pull the sheaths apart to separate the fibres, then the pith is scraped off using a fresh-water mussel shell. The fibre is so strong that it wears grooves into the shell during this process. Using these fibres the bag is woven, beginning at the bottom and working towards the top. At the top the ends of the fibres are sealed with wax from a native beehive, then bound with lawyer cane to form a neat rim. To complete the dillybag a lawyer-cane handle is attached to the top of the bag.

'JARRUKA' THE SCRUB HEN

Scrub hen eggs are good food for the Aborigines. The scrub hen makes a large nest, a mound of leaves and sticks up to about three metres high and seven metres across, in which she lays her eggs. The rotting vegetation generates heat and acts as an incubator.

Each year, at the beginning of winter, the women make special dillybags called 'jilnga' which are used for collecting and carrying the eggs. Unlike other dillybags, jilnga is woven from a particular type of grass which grows along the river banks. This grass has a waxy surface making it slippery and difficult to handle. To prepare the grass for weaving, it is drawn through the flames of a fire to burn off the wax. Then, using a sharp stick, each strand of grass is split into a number of thin strips which are woven into a bag. The dillybag is made to hold five eggs, the maximum number laid by the scrub hen at one time.

Scrub hen eggs have thin shells and must be handled carefully to avoid breakage while carrying them home. This is done by wrapping them individually in lawyer-cane leaves. Lawyer-cane leaves contain small hairs on their undersides and these provide a cushioning effect against the egg. The wrapped eggs are then placed in the dillybag and the soft texture of the bag fits around the eggs to give further protection.

Eggs are prepared for eating by baking them in the coals of a fire or by boiling them in a bark container called a 'dubal' over the fire. Scrub hen eggs are eaten at all stages of incubation.

GLOSSARY

~~~~~~

Some phonetics of the Kuku-Yalanji alphabet are slightly different from those used in the English language. The stress is placed on the first and third syllable.

a as in father	rr as in Scottish rolled r
i as in pit	ng as in sing
u as in put	k as a hard g as in gate

Word	Pronunciation	Meaning
balji	baal–ge	dillybag made from black palm
balur	bar–lor	fishing woomera
bujilnga	buge–ill–inga	emergency woomera
dubal	du–baal	bark container
durral	do–rr–al	spear-stick tree or fire-stick tree
duwar	doo–waa	hunting spear or man spear made from black palm
duwar	doo–waa	black palm
Jarruka	Jarr–oo–ga	scrub hen
jidu	gee–doo	wild ginger fruit (red)
jilnga	jil–nga	dillybag
jimal	gee–mal	fire sticks
jirimandi	gee–rr–e–mun–de	coconut
jujabala	joo–ja–bar–la	ironwood tree
jun jun	joon–joon	wild ginger fruit (green)

~~~~~~~~~~~

Word	Pronunciation	Meaning
kalka	gal–ga	fish spear
kambar	gum–ba–r	edible clay
Kumbi	Gum–be	flying fox
Kuku-Yalanji	Goo–goo–yal–an–gee	tribal name
Kurrmaja	Goo–rr–mar–ja	green ant drone
Maladikarra	Mala–dig–a–r	expert spear fighter
marra	marr–a	macrozamia nuts
milbar	mil–ba–r	fighting or hunting woomera
milbayarr	mil–bay–arr	woomera
mili	mil–ee	stinging tree
Ngawiya	Ngar–we–ya	turtle
Walmbaji	Wal–m–ba–gee	peacemaker
wangal	wang–al	boomerang
wukay	oog–ay	hairy yam
wurun	oo–roon	traditional shelter
Yangka	Young–ga	green ants
Yawu	Yar–oo	stingray
yiki yiki	eege–eege	didgeridoo